"It's hard to connect with your child without first understanding where they are. As counselors and speakers at parenting events across the country, we spend a great deal of time teaching parents about development. To know *where* your child is—not just physically, but emotionally, socially, and spiritually, helps you to truly know and understand *who* your child is. And that understanding is the key to connecting. The Phase Guides give you the tools to do just that. Our wise friends Reggie and Kristen have put together an insightful, hopeful, practical, and literal year-by-year guide that will help you to understand and connect with your child at every age."

SISSY GOFF
M.ED., LPC-MHSP, DIRECTOR OF CHILD & ADOLESCENT COUNSELING AT DAYSTAR COUNSELING MINISTRIES IN NASHVILLE, TENNESSEE, SPEAKER AND AUTHOR OF ARE MY KIDS ON TRACK?

"These resources for parents are fantastically empowering, absolute in their simplicity, and completely doable in every way. The hard work that has gone into the Phase Project will echo through the next generation of children in powerful ways."

JENNIFER WALKER
RN BSN, AUTHOR AND FOUNDER OF MOMS ON CALL

"We all know where we want to end up in our parenting, but how to get there can seem like an unsolved mystery. Through the Phase Project series, Reggie Joiner and Kristen Ivy team up to help us out. The result is a resource that guides us through the different seasons of raising children, and provides a road map to parenting in such a way that we finish up with very few regrets."

SANDRA STANLEY
FOSTER CARE ADVOCATE, BLOGGER, WIFE TO ANDY STANLEY, MOTHER OF THREE

"Not only are the Phase Guides the most creative and well-thought-out guides to parenting I have ever encountered, these books are ESSENTIAL to my daily parenting. With a 13-year-old, 11-year-old, and 9-year-old at home, I am swimming in their wake of daily drama and delicacy. These books are a reminder to enjoy every second. Because it's just a phase."

CARLOS WHITTAKER
AUTHOR, SPEAKER, FATHER OF THREE

"As the founder of Minnie's Food Pantry, I see thousands of people each month with children who will benefit from the advice, guidance, and nuggets of information on how to celebrate and understand the phases of their child's life. Too often we feel like we're losing our mind when sweet little Johnny starts to change his behavior into a person we do not know. I can't wait to start implementing the principles of these books with my clients to remind them . . . it's just a phase."

CHERYL JACKSON
FOUNDER OF MINNIE'S FOOD PANTRY, AWARD-WINNING PHILANTHROPIST, AND GRANDMOTHER

"I began exploring this resource with my counselor hat on, thinking how valuable this will be for the many parents I spend time with in my office. I ended up taking my counselor hat off and putting on my parent hat. Then I kept thinking about friends who are teachers, coaches, youth pastors, and children's ministers, who would want this in their hands. What a valuable resource the Orange team has given us to better understand and care for the kids and adolescents we love. I look forward to sharing it broadly."

DAVID THOMAS
LMSW, DIRECTOR OF FAMILY COUNSELING, DAYSTAR COUNSELING MINISTRIES, SPEAKER AND AUTHOR OF ARE MY KIDS ON TRACK? *AND* WILD THINGS: THE ART OF NURTURING BOYS

"I have always wished someone would hand me a manual for parenting. Well, the Phase Guides are more than what I wished for. They guide, inspire, and challenge me as a parent—while giving me incredible insight into my children at each age and phase. Our family will be using these every year!"

COURTNEY DEFEO
AUTHOR OF IN THIS HOUSE, WE WILL GIGGLE, *MOTHER OF TWO*

"As I speak to high school students and their parents, I always wonder to myself: What would it have been like if they had better seen what was coming next? What if they had a guide that would tell them what to expect and how to be ready? What if they could anticipate what is predictable about the high school years before they actually hit? These Phase Guides give a parent that kind of preparation so they can have a plan when they need it most."

JOSH SHIPP
AUTHOR, TEEN EXPERT, AND YOUTH SPEAKER

"The Phase Guides are incredibly creative, well researched, and filled with inspirational actions for everyday life. Each age-specific guide is catalytic for equipping parents to lead and love their kids as they grow up. I'm blown away and deeply encouraged by the content and by its creators. I highly recommend Phase resources for all parents, teachers, and influencers of children. This is the stuff that challenges us and changes our world. Get them. Read them. And use them!"

DANIELLE STRICKLAND
OFFICER WITH THE SALVATION ARMY, AUTHOR, SPEAKER, MOTHER OF TWO

"It's true that parenting is one of life's greatest joys but it is not without its challenges. If we're honest, parenting can sometimes feel like trying to choreograph a dance to an ever-changing beat. It can be clumsy and riddled with well-meaning missteps. If parenting is a dance, this Parenting Guide is a skilled instructor refining your technique and helping you move gracefully to a steady beat. For those of us who love to plan ahead, this guide will help you anticipate what's to come so you can be poised and ready to embrace the moments you want to enjoy."

TINA NAIDOO
MSSW, LCSW EXECUTIVE DIRECTOR, THE POTTER'S HOUSE OF DALLAS, INC.

PARENTING YOUR FOURTH GRADER

A GUIDE TO MAKING THE MOST OF THE "I'VE GOT THIS" PHASE

KRISTEN IVY AND REGGIE JOINER

PARENTING YOUR FOURTH GRADER
A GUIDE TO MAKING THE MOST OF THE
"I'VE GOT THIS" PHASE

Published by Orange, a division of The reThink Group, Inc.,
5870 Charlotte Lane, Suite 300,
Cumming, GA 30040 U.S.A.

©2017 The Phase Project
Authors: Kristen Ivy and Reggie Joiner
Lead Editor: Karen Wilson
Editing Team: Melanie Williams, Hannah Crosby, Sherry Surratt

Art Direction: Ryan Boon and Hannah Crosby
Book Design: FiveStone and Sharon van Rossum
Project Manager : Nate Brandt

Printed in the United States of America
First Edition 2017
6 7 8 9 10 11 12 13 14 15

10/15/2018

Special thanks to:

*Jim Burns, Ph.D for guidance and consultation
on having conversations about sexual integrity*

*Jon Acuff for guidance and consultation on having
conversations about technological responsibility*

*Jean Sumner, MD for guidance and consultation
on having conversations about healthy habits*

*Every educator, counselor, community leader, and
researcher who invested in the Phase Project*

TABLE OF CONTENTS

HOW TO USE THIS ~~BOOK~~ ~~JOURNAL~~ GUIDE

The guide you hold in your hand doesn't have very many words, but it does have a lot of ideas. Some of these ideas come from thousands of hours of research. Others come from parents, educators, and volunteers who spend every day with kids the same age as yours. This guide won't tell you everything about your kid, but it will tell you a few things about kids at this age.

The best way to use this guide is to take what these pages tell you about fourth graders and combine it with what you know is true about *your* fourth grader.

Let's sum it up:

THINGS ABOUT FOURTH GRADERS +
THOUGHTS ABOUT *YOUR* FOURTH GRADER =
YOUR GUIDE TO THE NEXT 52 WEEKS OF PARENTING

After each idea in this guide, there are pages with a few questions designed to prompt you to think about your kid, your family, and yourself as a parent. The only guarantee we give to parents who use this guide is this: You will mess up some things as a parent this year. Actually, that's a guarantee to every parent, regardless. But you, you picked up this book! You want to be a better parent. And that's what we hope this guide will do: help you parent your kid just a little better, simply because you paused to consider a few ideas that can help you make the most of this phase.

THE FOURTH GRADE PHASE

There's something magical about the fourth grade. Okay, maybe *magical* isn't the right word. But I simply can't find another word to sum up the incomprehensible value of this phase.

Early in my career, I remember having a conversation with Bobb Biehl that really solidified my belief in the importance of the fourth grade. Bobb was the president of a master-planning group. He had never worked with children. Instead, he worked with executives and CEOs. The first time Bobb and I sat down to have a conversation about business and leadership, he began with this question: "Can you tell me about what happened when you were in the fourth grade?"

I was a little taken aback. It certainly wasn't the question I had been expecting. But then Bobb went on to say that the fourth grade is the *most* deciding time in a person's life.

Throughout the rest of my career, I've been fascinated by the significance of the fourth grade. If you ask most adults to recall a memory from childhood, to reach back to their earliest long-term memory, the vast majority will tell you something that happened in the fourth grade.

Since I work in sports, I often ask grown men this question: "When you played football in the fourth grade, which position did you play?" The ironic thing to me is that most men answer that question by giving me a position. In truth, most fourth grade teams rotate players so everyone will play all positions. But what a person remembers playing is often an indication of how they felt about their value to the team.

What a kid believes about themselves in the fourth grade matters. It leaves a lasting memory—one that will form a long-term belief about how they see themselves.

Later, Bobb and I would write the book *Every Child Is a Winner*, where we worked to highlight the potential of this phase. We included a section to explain how most children grow from an early belief that "everybody is just like me," into the realization that "hey, everybody is not just like me," and finally (around the fourth grade), into the discovery that "there's nobody just like me."

The troubling thing about this fourth grade realization is that it comes with a whole lot of other questions. Fourth graders often wonder: "Is something wrong with me?" And, unless a fourth grader hears consistent voices to re-affirm their value, they may become stuck in this struggle.

Here's where you, the parent, come in. Now is your moment to get on their level, eye-to-eye, and consistently communicate: "There is nobody just like you, and that's just the way it should be. You are exactly the way God made you."

It may seem like this isn't the phase to emphasize your influence as a parent. After all, your fourth grader may be spending more and more time around their friends. Or they may be withdrawing and discovering they enjoy time alone working on a hobby or skill. It may seem as if you're losing influence. But don't be fooled. Your fourth grader needs you as much as ever.

There will never be another year quite like this one. Don't let it rush past you. And resist the temptation to hurry forward into the next phase. Simply sink into fourth grade and make the most of this remarkably unique and formative phase.

- CAZ MCCASLIN
FOUNDER AND PRESIDENT OF UPWARD SPORTS

52
WEEKS
—
TO PARENT YOUR
FOURTH GRADER

WHEN YOU SEE
HOW MUCH

Time

YOU HAVE LEFT

———

YOU TEND TO DO

More

WITH THE TIME
YOU HAVE NOW.

THERE ARE APPROXIMATELY

936 WEEKS

FROM THE TIME A BABY IS BORN UNTIL THEY GROW UP AND MOVE TO WHATEVER IS NEXT.

On the day your child starts fourth grade, you only have 468 weeks remaining. That means you are halfway to graduation, or at least halfway to having a kid who can legally serve jury duty. The weeks ahead will move much more quickly than the first 468, and you're well aware your kid is growing up—fast.

That's why every week counts. Of course, each week might not feel significant. There may be weeks this year when all you feel like you accomplished was surviving a fourth-grade sleepover. That's okay.

Take a deep breath.
You don't have to get everything done this week.

But what happens in your child's life week after week, year after year, adds up over time. So, it might be a good idea to put a number to your weeks.

MEASURE IT OUT.

Write down the number of weeks that have already passed since your kid was born. Then write down the number of weeks you have left before they graduate high school.

HINT: If you want a little help counting it out, you can download the free Parent Cue app on all mobile platforms.

CREATE A VISUAL COUNTDOWN.

Find a jar and fill it with one marble for each week you have remaining with your child. Then make a habit of removing one marble every week as a reminder to make the most of your time. Where can you place your visual countdown so you will see it frequently?

Which day of the week is best for you to remove a marble?

_____

_____

_____

Is there anything you want to do each week as you remove
a marble? *(Examples: say a prayer, play a game, retell one
favorite memory from this past week)*

_____

_____

_____

_____

_____

_____

_____

_____

_____

_____

_____

_____

EVERY PHASE IS A

TIMEFRAME

IN A KID'S LIFE

WHEN YOU CAN

LEVERAGE

DISTINCTIVE

OPPORTUNITIES

TO INFLUENCE

THEIR

future.

YOU ONLY HAVE
52 WEEKS
WITH YOUR FOURTH GRADER

while they are still in fourth grade.

Then they will be in fifth grade,

and you will never know them as a fourth grader again.

Or, to say it another way:

Before you know it, your kid will grow up a little more and . . . .

have a secret crush.

have a few mood swings.

beg for a cell phone (if they haven't already).

The point is this: The phase you are in now has remarkable potential.
And before the end of fourth grade, there are some distinctive
opportunities you don't want to miss. So, as you count down the
next 52 weeks, pay attention to what makes these weeks uniquely
different from the time you've already spent together and the weeks
you will have when they move on to the next phase.

What are some things you have noticed about your fourth grader in this phase that you really enjoy?

_____

_____

_____

_____

_____

_____

_____

_____

_____

_____

_____

_____

_____

_____

_____

_____

_____

_____

_____

_____

What is something new you are learning as a parent during this phase?

_____

_____

_____

_____

_____

_____

_____

_____

_____

_____

_____

_____

_____

_____

_____

_____

_____

_____

_____

_____

FOURTH GRADE

—

THE PHASE WHEN FRIENDS ARE BEST FRIENDS, GAMES ARE FOR COMPETITION, AND YOUR CONFIDENT KID WILL INSIST,

"I've got this."

FRIENDS MATTER MORE.

Fourth grade friend-groups may be quickly turning into cliques, and friendships may evolve into "best friends." Look for ways to fuel healthy friendships. They are the perfect place to learn some of life's most valuable skills.

COMPETITION CAN BE FUN.

With a "lifetime" of practice under their belt, your fourth grader is ready to prove they can win. Almost nothing motivates a fourth grader more than a good competition. It's one way to show you how smart and fast and strong they really are. But since the outcome typically matters more than the game (to them), you might be on the lookout for a few negotiations and rule changes along the way.

NATURAL CONFIDENCE RULES.

It's the fifth year of school, and your kid has this routine down. So on the days when your kid may be feeling anxious or worried, ask what you can do to help. Encourage persistence over performance, and constantly remind them, "You've got this." They are gaining the confidence they will need for the phases to come.

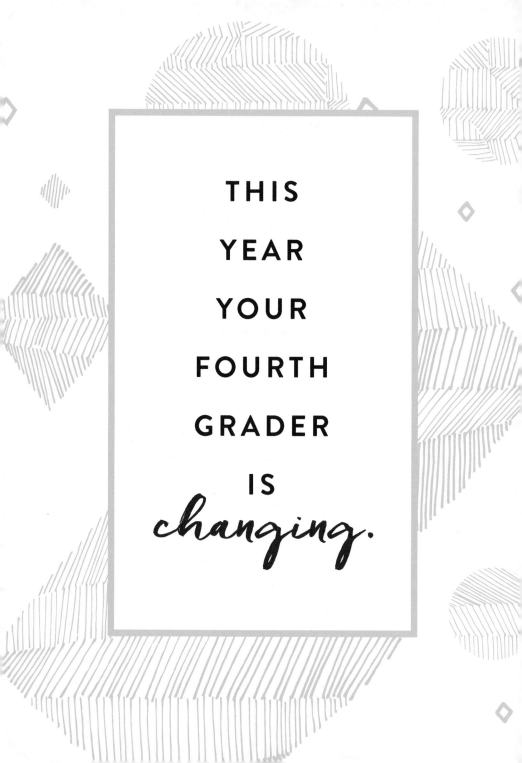

THIS
YEAR
YOUR
FOURTH
GRADER
IS
changing.

PHYSICALLY

- Continues losing baby teeth including molars (9-12 years)

- Improves in speed, force, and body control

- Needs physical activity and may become restless

- May show signs of early stages of puberty: acne, mood swings, changes in weight and height (girls 8-9, boys 9-12 years)

- Needs 10-11 hours of sleep each night

MENTALLY

- Can focus on one activity for 45 minutes

- Can read silently and remember what they've read

- Able to collaborate on rules and consequences

- Recognizes different perspectives and becoming more empathetic

- Still struggles with abstract concepts

SOCIALLY

- Increasingly values peer approval

- Desires more personal privacy

- Often thrives in competitive situations

- Benefits from having a same-gender best friend

- May be interested in or curious about opposite-gender relationships (but rarely admit it)

EMOTIONALLY

- Frequently exhibits signs of anxiety

- May begin to be embarrassed about their body

- Enjoys puns, sarcasm, and sometimes crude jokes

- Still holds to family beliefs and values, but may ask challenging questions

- May be drawn to a humanitarian cause and enjoy service opportunities

What are some changes you are noticing in your fourth grader?

_____

_____

_____

_____

_____

_____

_____

You may disagree with some of the characteristics we've shared about fourth graders. That's because every fourth grader is unique. What makes your fourth grader different from fourth graders in general?

_____

_____

_____

_____

_____

_____

_____

_____

What do you want to remember about this year with your fourth grader?

Mark this page. Throughout the year, write down a few simple things you want to remember. If you want to be really thorough, there are about 52 blank lines. But some weeks, you may spend so much time trying to decode their new top-secret language that you forget to write down a memory. That's okay.

_____

_____

_____

_____

_____

_____

_____

_____

_____

_____

_____

_____

_____

_____

SIX THINGS

—

EVERY KID

NEEDS

YOUR KID **NEEDS 6 THINGS OVER TIME**

LOVE

WORDS

WORK

TRIBES

STORIES

FUN

OVER THE NEXT 468 WEEKS, YOUR CHILD WILL NEED MANY THINGS:

Some of the things your kid needs will change from phase to phase, but there are six things every kid needs at every phase. In fact, these things may be the most important things you give your kid.

EVERY KID, AT EVERY PHASE, NEEDS . . .

♡ LOVE
to give them a
sense of WORTH.

📖 STORIES
to give them a bigger
PERSPECTIVE.

🏋 WORK
to give them
SIGNIFICANCE.

♟ FUN
to give them
CONNECTION.

👥 TRIBES
to give them
BELONGING.

💬 WORDS
to give them
DIRECTION.

The next few pages are designed to help you think about how you will give your child these six things, right now—while they are in fourth grade.

EVERY KID

NEEDS

love

OVER TIME

—

TO GIVE THEM

A SENSE OF

worth.

ONE QUESTION YOUR FOURTH GRADER IS ASKING

Your fourth grader can understand different points of view, empathize with others, and negotiate like a champ. That means one thing: Your influence is shifting. Your kid still needs you, but they are beginning to need you in a different way.

Your fourth grader is asking one major question:

"DO I HAVE FRIENDS?"

Sure, everyone needs a friend. But research shows there's extraordinary value in having a best friend in the fourth grade. Kids need to share their most authentic version of themselves with another person. So, give your fourth grader the love and acceptance they need by doing one thing:

ENGAGE their interests.

And remember, they are interested in friends. So, this year include peers, coach relational skills, and help them develop healthy friendships. When you engage your fourth grader's interests, you communicate, "Your relationships have value."

You are probably doing more for your fourth grader than your fourth grader gives you credit for. (So it's a good thing you didn't get into this parenting game for all the approval and recognition.) Make a list of the ways you already show up consistently to engage your fourth grader's interests.

You may need to look at this list on a bad day to remember what a great parent you are.

_____

_____

_____

_____

_____

_____

_____

_____

_____

_____

_____

_____

_____

_____

Engaging your child's interests requires paying attention to what they like. What does your fourth grader seem to enjoy the most right now?

It's impossible to love anyone with the often-unacknowledged effort a fourth grader requires unless you have a little time for yourself. What can you do to refuel each week so you are able to give your fourth grader the love they need?

Who do you have around you supporting you this year?

_____

_____

_____

_____

_____

_____

_____

_____

_____

_____

_____

_____

_____

_____

_____

_____

_____

_____

_____

_____

EVERY KID

NEEDS

stories

OVER TIME

—

TO GIVE THEM

A BIGGER

perspective.

BOOKS TO READ
WITH YOUR FOURTH GRADER

THE INDIAN IN THE CUPBOARD
by Lynn Reid Banks

EL DEAFO
by Cece Bell

LOVE THAT DOG
by Sharon Creech

WALK TWO MOONS
by Sharon Creech

HOW TO TRAIN YOUR DRAGON (SERIES)
by Cressida Cowell

THE BLACK STALLION
by Walter Farley

MY SIDE OF THE MOUNTAIN
by Jean Craighead George

DIARY OF A WIMPY KID (SERIES)
by Jeff Kinney

THE CHRONICLES OF NARNIA (SERIES)
by C. S. Lewis

ANNE OF GREEN GABLES (SERIES)
by L. M. Montgomery

THE BORROWERS
by Mary Norton

BIG NATE (SERIES)
by Lincoln Peirce

PAX
by Sara Pennypacker

SHILOH
by Phyllis Reynolds Naylor

WHERE THE RED FERN GROWS
by Wilson Rawls

PERCY JACKSON (SERIES)
by Rick Riordan

HARRY POTTER (BOOKS 4-5)
by J. K. Rowling

THE INVENTION OF HUGO CABRET
by Brian Selznick

WONDERSTRUCK
by Brian Selznick

I SURVIVED (SERIES)
by Lauren Tarshis

Tell your fourth grader's story. What are some moments you want to re-tell?

Think of times you saw your fourth grader doing something good, times you both learned something new, or maybe a special time when you had fun together.

_____

_____

_____

_____

_____

_____

_____

_____

_____

_____

_____

_____

_____

_____

_____

_____

How might you share grandparent or great-grandparent stories with your fourth grader? If you have an adopted or foster child, how might you talk about and celebrate your child's ancestral family?

_____

_____

_____

_____

_____

_____

_____

_____

_____

_____

_____

_____

_____

_____

_____

_____

_____

_____

_____

Tell your family story. What do you want to record now so you can share it with your fourth grader later? Consider starting a family journal, a video archive, a travel scrapbook, or a drawer of things connected to special memories. Write down some ideas that might fit your family's values and style.

_____

_____

_____

_____

_____

_____

_____

_____

_____

_____

_____

_____

_____

_____

_____

_____

EVERY KID

NEEDS

work

OVER TIME

—

TO GIVE

THEM

significance.

WORK YOUR
FOURTH GRADER CAN DO

TAKE TEMPERATURE
(but you might check it)

CLIP FINGERNAILS

READ TO YOUNGER CHILDREN

DO HOMEWORK

PLANT OR PET SIT FOR NEIGHBORS

LOAD AND UNLOAD THE DISHWASHER

VACUUM CARPET

CLEAN THE BATHROOM

WIPE DOWN MIRRORS AND WINDOWS

SORT, WASH, FOLD, AND PUT AWAY LAUNDRY

USE A HAMMER

CHANGE BED SHEETS, MAKE THE BED, AND CLEAN THEIR ROOM
(even if it doesn't always stay that way)

What are some jobs you can give to your fourth grader?

_____

_____

_____

_____

_____

_____

_____

_____

_____

_____

_____

_____

_____

_____

_____

_____

_____

_____

_____

_____

_____

_____

Some days it's easier than others to motivate your fourth grader to do their work. What are some strategies that tend to keep your fourth grader motivated?

🔑 **HINT**: Maybe try a few things like, "You can choose the movie/ game for Friday night."

_____

_____

_____

_____

_____

_____

_____

_____

_____

_____

_____

_____

_____

_____

_____

_____

What are things you hope your fourth grader will be able to do independently in the next phase?

How are you helping them develop those skills now?

_____

_____

_____

_____

_____

_____

_____

_____

_____

_____

_____

_____

_____

_____

_____

_____

_____

_____

_____

_____

_____

_____

_____

EVERY KID

NEEDS

fun

OVER TIME

—

TO GIVE

THEM

connection.

WAYS TO HAVE FUN
WITH YOUR FOURTH GRADER

GAMES:

CLUE®	PICTIONARY®	ARE YOU SMARTER THAN A 5TH GRADER?®
MONOPOLY®	CHESS	
MANCALA	THE GAME OF LIFE®	TICKET TO RIDE®
QUIRKLE®	CATAN®	MASTERMIND®
SCRABBLE®	FARKLE®	HEADS UP®

ACTIVITIES:

DRAW / PAINT	SARDINES (when friends come over)	WATER GAMES (Marco Polo)
MAKE JEWELRY / BUILD MODELS		EVENTS AT THE LIBRARY
H.O.R.S.E. (Basketball)	RAGE, HIT THE DECK, SPOONS (card games)	100+ PIECE JIGSAW PUZZLES
FOUR SQUARE	HANGMAN	HONEY, I LOVE YOU, BUT I JUST CAN'T SMILE
CORN HOLE	MAD LIBS®	
CAPTURE THE FLAG	LEGOS®	DOTS
CHARADES	LOCAL MUSEUMS	
PAPER FOOTBALL		

What are some games and activities you and your fourth grader enjoy?

_____

_____

_____

_____

_____

_____

_____

_____

_____

_____

_____

_____

_____

_____

_____

_____

_____

_____

_____

_____

_____

When are the best times of the day, or week, for you to set
aside to just have fun with your fourth grader?

_____

_____

_____

_____

_____

_____

_____

_____

_____

_____

_____

_____

_____

_____

_____

_____

_____

_____

_____

Some days are *extra* fun days. What are some ways you want to celebrate the special days coming up this year?

CHILD'S BIRTHDAY

_____

_____

_____

_____

_____

_____

_____

_____

_____

_____

_____

_____

_____

_____

_____

_____

HOLIDAYS

_____

_____

_____

_____

_____

_____

_____

_____

_____

_____

_____

_____

_____

_____

_____

_____

_____

_____

_____

_____

_____

_____

_____

_____

_____

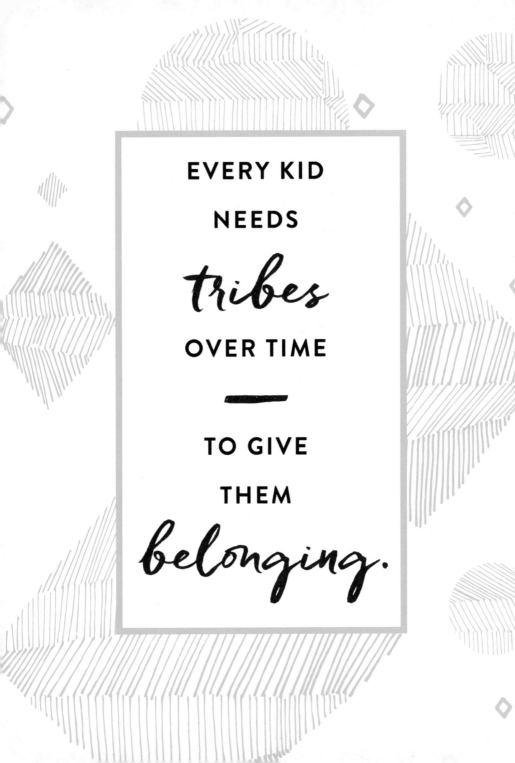

EVERY KID

NEEDS

tribes

OVER TIME

—

TO GIVE

THEM

belonging.

ADULTS WHO MIGHT INFLUENCE YOUR FOURTH GRADER

PARENTS

NEIGHBORS

CHURCH LEADERS

GRANDPARENTS

PARENT'S FRIENDS

COACHES

AUNTS & UNCLES

FOURTH GRADE TEACHER

SCHOOL WORKERS

List at least five adults who have influence in your fourth grader's life right now.

HINT: If you aren't sure, you can ask them.

_____

_____

_____

_____

_____

_____

_____

_____

_____

_____

_____

_____

_____

_____

_____

_____

_____

_____

_____

What is one way these adults could help you and your fourth grader this year?

_____

_____

_____

_____

_____

_____

_____

_____

_____

_____

_____

_____

_____

_____

_____

_____

_____

_____

What are a few ways you could show these adults appreciation for the significant role they play in your child's life?

EVERY KID

NEEDS

words

OVER TIME

—

TO GIVE

THEM

direction.

WORDS YOUR FOURTH GRADER NEEDS TO HEAR

GOOD MORNING!

I LOVE YOU

TELL ME MORE

I HOPE YOU KNOW . . .

I HAVE NOTICED . . .

BE KIND

I'M SORRY

I'M REALLY PROUD WHEN . . .

I ENJOY SPENDING TIME WITH YOU

WORK HARD

WANT A HUG?

KEEP TRYING

YOU ARE BEAUTIFUL / HANDSOME

I'VE BEEN THINKING . . .

GOOD NIGHT!

I CAN ALWAYS COUNT ON YOU TO . . .

If words over time give a kid direction, what word (or words) describes your hopes for your fourth grader in this phase?

DETERMINED	MOTIVATED	GENTLE
ENCOURAGING	INTROSPECTIVE	PASSIONATE
SELF-ASSURED	ENTHUSIASTIC	PATIENT
ASSERTIVE	JOYFUL	FORGIVING
DARING	ENTERTAINING	CREATIVE
INSIGHTFUL	INDEPENDENT	WITTY
COMPASSIONATE	OBSERVANT	AMBITIOUS
AMIABLE	SENSITIVE	HELPFUL
EASY-GOING	ENDEARING	AUTHENTIC
DILIGENT	ADVENTUROUS	INVENTIVE
PROACTIVE	HONEST	DEVOTED
OPTIMISTIC	CURIOUS	GENUINE
FEARLESS	DEPENDABLE	ATTENTIVE
AFFECTIONATE	GENEROUS	HARMONIOUS
COURAGEOUS	COMMITTED	EMPATHETIC
CAUTIOUS	RESPONSIBLE	COURAGEOUS
DEVOTED	TRUSTWORTHY	FLEXIBLE
INQUISITIVE	THOUGHTFUL	CAREFUL
PATIENT	LOYAL	NURTURING
OPEN-MINDED	KIND	RELIABLE

Where can you place those words in your home so they will remind you what you want for your child this year?

_____

_____

_____

_____

_____

_____

_____

_____

_____

_____

_____

_____

_____

_____

_____

_____

_____

_____

_____

_____

The words we use determine the way we think. Are there words you have chosen not to say (or not to say often)? What do you want for your kid to know about these words, and how do you want them to respond if they hear them?

_____

_____

_____

_____

_____

_____

_____

_____

_____

_____

_____

_____

_____

_____

_____

_____

_____

_____
_____
_____
_____
_____
_____
_____
_____
_____
_____
_____
_____
_____
_____
_____
_____
_____
_____
_____
_____
_____
_____
_____
_____
_____

FOUR
CONVERSATIONS

—

TO HAVE IN THIS
PHASE

WHEN YOU KNOW
WHERE YOU WANT
TO GO,

AND YOU KNOW
WHERE YOU ARE
NOW,

YOU CAN ALWAYS
DO SOMETHING

TO MOVE IN A
BETTER DIRECTION.

→

OVER THE NEXT 468 WEEKS OF YOUR CHILD'S LIFE, SOME CONVERSATIONS MAY MATTER MORE THAN OTHERS.

WHAT YOU SAY, FOR EXAMPLE, REGARDING . . .
Star Wars
Shark attacks
and Justin Timberlake

MIGHT HAVE LESS IMPACT ON THEIR FUTURE THAN WHAT YOU SAY REGARDING . . .
Health
Sex
Technology
or Faith.

The next pages are about the conversations that matter most. On the left page is a destination—what you might want to be true in your kid's life 468 weeks from now. On the right page is a goal for conversations with your fourth grader and a few suggestions about what you might want to say.

Healthy habits

—

LEARNING TO STRENGTHEN MY BODY THROUGH EXERCISE, NUTRITION, AND SELF-ADVOCACY

THIS YEAR YOU WILL

DEVELOP POSITIVE ROUTINES

SO YOUR CHILD WILL ENJOY EATING WELL

AND EXERCISING OFTEN.

Maintain a good relationship with your pediatrician, and schedule a well visit at least once per year. You can also begin to develop healthy habits for your fourth grader with a few simple words.

SAY THINGS LIKE . . .

I LOVE TO WATCH YOU PLAY!

"WOULD YOU GO ON A RUN WITH ME?"

TIME FOR BED!
(Preteens need 10-11 hours of sleep.)

"I'M NOT SURE DRINKING SODA MAKES YOU LOOK LIKE THAT."
(Talk about advertisements and body image.)

"WHAT HAVE YOU HEARD ABOUT MARIJUANA?"
(Begin talking about drugs and alcohol.)

FOR GIRLS: "SOMETIMES BEFORE YOUR PERIOD, YOUR UTERUS MUSCLES START TO ACHE."
(If you haven't already, talk about things like PMS, cramps, or what to do when you get your period at school.)

"ALMONDS HAVE HEALTHY FAT THAT YOUR BODY NEEDS."
(Teach the importance of eating the right types of foods.)

What are some activities you can do with your fourth grader that require a little bit of exercise? *(They may not call it exercise, but if you get a little winded that counts.)*

_____

_____

_____

_____

_____

_____

_____

_____

_____

_____

_____

_____

_____

_____

_____

_____

_____

_____

_____

Kids who cook learn about what ingredients are in the things they eat. What are some simple ways your fourth grader can help you in the kitchen?

_____

_____

_____

_____

_____

_____

_____

_____

_____

_____

_____

_____

_____

_____

_____

_____

_____

Who will help you monitor and improve your fourth
grader's health?

_____

_____

_____

_____

_____

_____

_____

_____

_____

_____

_____

_____

_____

_____

_____

_____

_____

_____

What are your own health goals for this year? How can you improve the habits in your own life—*you know, even if the occasional fourth grade sleepover party makes you break all diet, sleep, and exercise routines?*

_____

_____

_____

_____

_____

_____

_____

_____

_____

_____

_____

_____

_____

_____

_____

_____

_____

_____

Sexual integrity

—

GUARDING MY
POTENTIAL FOR
INTIMACY THROUGH
APPROPRIATE
BOUNDARIES
AND MUTUAL
RESPECT

THIS YEAR YOU WILL

INFORM THEM ABOUT HOW THINGS WORK

SO YOUR CHILD WILL UNDERSTAND BIOLOGY
AND BUILD SOCIAL SKILLS.

Your fourth grader is in a perfect phase for conversations about sexual integrity. Fourth graders are beginning to experience body changes (or have friends who are), so these conversations feel personally relevant. And a fourth grader still holds strongly to family values, so they believe that what you tell them is true, is true.

SAY THINGS LIKE . . .

"I'M SO GLAD YOU ASKED ME."

"CAN WE TALK MORE ABOUT THIS ANOTHER TIME?"
(Always finish the conversation with room to pick it back up again later.)

"PORNOGRAPHY IS DANGEROUS BECAUSE IT OFTEN BECOMES AN ADDICTION THAT CAN LIMIT YOUR ABILITY TO ENJOY REAL SEX LATER."
(Talk about why pornography can be harmful.)

"SEX CAN BE DANGEROUS OUTSIDE OF MARRIAGE."
(Caution sexual activity.)

I DON'T LIKE TO HEAR SOMEONE SAY THAT WORD BECAUSE . . .
(Refine the words they use for bodies, sex, and people.)

WHAT KINDS OF THINGS HAVE YOU HEARD ABOUT SEX?

"WHERE DID YOU HEAR ABOUT . . . ?"

"WHAT DO YOU THINK THAT MEANS?"

"YOU ARE BEAUTIFUL / HANDSOME JUST THE WAY YOU ARE."

When it comes to your child's sexuality, what do you hope is true for them 468 weeks from now?

_____

_____

_____

_____

_____

_____

_____

_____

_____

_____

_____

_____

_____

_____

_____

_____

_____

_____

_____

_____

_____

Write down a few things you want to communicate to your fourth grader about body changes, sex, pornography, and respect for themselves and others. *(You don't have to tell them everything now, or in one talk. This should be many talks— over time.)*

_____

_____

_____

_____

_____

_____

_____

_____

_____

_____

_____

_____

_____

_____

_____

_____

_____

_____

Follow up. Anytime you talk to your fourth grader about sex, you may walk away feeling like there were things you didn't say that you wish you would have said, or things you said that you wish you had said better. Use this space to reflect. What do you want to communicate better next time?

_____

_____

_____

_____

_____

_____

_____

_____

_____

_____

_____

_____

_____

_____

_____

_____

Technological responsibility

—

LEVERAGING THE POTENTIAL OF ONLINE EXPERIENCES TO ENHANCE MY OFFLINE COMMUNITY AND SUCCESS

THIS YEAR YOU WILL

EXPLORE THE POSSIBILITIES

SO YOUR CHILD WILL UNDERSTAND CORE VALUES AND BUILD ONLINE SKILLS.

It may be getting harder to keep up with everything your fourth grader knows when it comes to digital devices, online games, apps, and software systems. Don't fall back. Press in. Let your fourth grader teach you all the wonderful ways they are learning to use technology.

SAY THINGS LIKE . . .

"WHAT DO YOU THINK IS A HEALTHY AMOUNT OF TIME ONLINE?"
(Collaborate on expectations, rules, and consequences.)

"CAN YOU HELP ME FIGURE OUT HOW TO . . . "

"TELL ME MORE ABOUT HOW THAT WORKS."

"HAVE YOU EVER SEEN SOMEONE SAY REALLY MEAN THINGS ONLINE?"

"LET ME FIND OUT MORE ABOUT THAT AND I WILL LET YOU KNOW."
(Look up things like age limits, content ratings, and connection to strangers.)

CAN WE PLAY TOGETHER?
(Make technology social by playing online games together.)

HAVE YOU SEEN ANYTHING ONLINE THAT SURPRISED YOU?

"WE SHOULD RESPECT PEOPLE ONLINE JUST AS MUCH AS WE RESPECT THEM IN PERSON."
(Talk about how devices sometimes escalate bullying).

"SOMETIMES PEOPLE PRETEND TO BE SOMEONE THEY AREN'T ONLINE."
(Caution against contact with strangers.)

When it comes to your child's engagement with technology, what do you hope is true for them 468 weeks from now?

_____

_____

_____

_____

_____

_____

_____

_____

_____

_____

_____

_____

_____

_____

_____

_____

_____

_____

_____

_____

_____

What rules do you have for digital devices in your family? If you don't have any, what are two or three you might want to set for your fourth grader?

_____

_____

_____

_____

_____

_____

_____

_____

_____

_____

_____

_____

_____

_____

_____

_____

_____

_____

What are your own personal values and disciplines when it comes to leveraging technology? Are there ways you want to improve your own savvy, skill, or responsibility in this area?

_____

_____

_____

_____

_____

_____

_____

_____

_____

_____

_____

_____

_____

_____

_____

_____

_____

_____

_____

LET'S TALK ABOUT THE PHONE.

They are probably already asking, and you may be digging in your heels. So, sometime when your fourth grader isn't around to pressure you, here are a few things to consider:

What are the honest pros and cons of giving your kid a phone?

_____

_____

_____

_____

_____

_____

_____

_____

_____

_____

_____

_____

_____

_____

_____

_____

When do you feel is the ideal age to give your kid a phone? *(You will need to know the answer as you negotiate with your fourth grader, because you can bet they know what they think the ideal age is.)*

_____

_____

_____

_____

_____

What are some ways you want to restrict the access on their phone initially?

If you aren't sure, check out our free cell phone guide at ParentCue.org/cellphoneguide. Or do a quick Google search for more ideas. Then write your own thoughts below.

_____

_____

_____

_____

_____

_____

How can you set expectations so your kid knows they can earn
more freedom over time?

_____

_____

_____

_____

_____

_____

_____

_____

_____

_____

_____

_____

_____

_____

_____

_____

_____

_____

_____

_____

_____

_____

Authentic faith

—

TRUSTING JESUS
IN A WAY THAT
TRANSFORMS HOW
I LOVE GOD,
MYSELF,
AND THE REST
OF THE WORLD

THIS YEAR YOU WILL
PROVOKE DISCOVERY
SO YOUR CHILD WILL TRUST GOD'S CHARACTER AND EXPERIENCE GOD'S FAMILY.

Fourth graders are often introspective and enjoy having some alone time. Leverage this new tendency to help them develop a habit of spending time alone with God. Help them pick out a preteen devotional, and continue having faith conversations at home.

SAY THINGS LIKE . . .

"HOW CAN I PRAY FOR YOU TODAY / THIS WEEK?"

"HAVING FAITH ISN'T ALWAYS EASY, BUT WE CAN TRUST GOD NO MATTER WHAT."

"WHAT DO YOU THINK IS THE WISEST CHOICE IN THIS SITUATION?"

"IF YOU WERE THEM, HOW DO YOU THINK YOU WOULD WANT TO BE TREATED?"

"HAVE YOU READ ANYTHING IN THE BIBLE THAT MEANS A LOT TO YOU RIGHT NOW?"
(Talk about the Bible.)

"AS FOR GOD, HIS WAY IS PERFECT: THE LORD'S WORD IS FLAWLESS, HE SHIELDS ALL WHO TAKE REFUGE IN HIM." Psalm 18:30
(Repeat simple Bible verses.)

"DID YOU KNOW THAT THE BIBLE WAS WRITTEN AS 66 DIFFERENT BOOKS, BUT THEY ALL TELL ONE STORY?"
(Connect the dots between the stories to give a bigger context.)

"I'VE BEEN WANTING TO VOLUNTEER MORE. IS THERE SOMEWHERE WE COULD SERVE TOGETHER?"
(Consider serving at your church or a local ministry that appeals to your kid's interests.)

When it comes to your kid's faith, what do you hope is true for them 468 weeks from now?

_____

_____

_____

_____

_____

_____

_____

_____

_____

_____

_____

_____

_____

_____

_____

_____

_____

_____

_____

_____

What adults are helping influence and develop your fourth grader's faith?

_____

_____

_____

_____

_____

_____

_____

_____

_____

_____

_____

_____

_____

_____

_____

_____

_____

_____

_____

_____

_____

What routines or habits do you have in your own life that are stretching your faith?

_____

_____

_____

_____

_____

_____

_____

_____

_____

_____

_____

_____

_____

_____

_____

_____

_____

_____

_____

THE

rhythm

OF YOUR

WEEK

—

WILL SHAPE

THE VALUES

IN YOUR

home.

NOW THAT YOU HAVE FILLED THIS BOOK WITH IDEAS AND GOALS, IT MAY SEEM AS IF YOU WILL NEVER HAVE TIME TO GET IT ALL DONE.

Actually, you have *468 weeks.*

And every week has potential.

The secret to making the most of this phase with your fourth grader is to take advantage of the time you already have. Create a rhythm to your weeks by leveraging these four times together.

Be a coach.
Instill purpose by starting the day with encouraging words.

Be a friend.
Interpret life during informal conversations as you travel.

Be a teacher.
Establish values with intentional conversations while you eat together.

Be a counselor.
Strengthen your relationship through heart conversations at the end of the day.

What are some of your favorite routines with your
fourth grader?

_____

_____

_____

_____

_____

_____

_____

_____

_____

_____

_____

_____

_____

_____

_____

_____

_____

_____

_____

Write down any other thoughts or questions you have about parenting your fourth grader.

_____

_____

_____

_____

_____

_____

_____

_____

_____

_____

_____

_____

_____

_____

_____

_____

_____

_____

_____

_____

_____

TO _LOVE GOD_

Provoke
discovery $\longrightarrow$ SO THEY WILL . . .
TRUST GOD'S CHARACTER
& EXPERIENCE GOD'S FAMILY

WISDOM
(First day of school)

FAITH
(Trust Jesus)

AY?

DO I HAVE YOUR ATTENTION?

DO I HAVE WHAT IT TAKES?

DO I HAVE FRIENDS?

K & FIRST

SECOND & THIRD

FOURTH & FIFTH

ENGAGE **their interests**

EVERY KID → MADE I
THE IMA
OF GO

Incite
wonder → SO THEY WILL . . .
KNOW GOD'S LOVE
& MEET GOD'S FAMILY

BEGINNING
(Baby dedication)

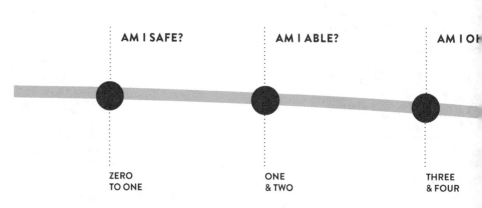

AM I SAFE?   AM I ABLE?   AM I OI

ZERO   ONE   THREE
TO ONE   & TWO   & FOUR

EMBRACE *their physical needs*

YOU HAVE

APPROXIMATELY

468 WEEKS.

_____

_____

_____

_____

_____

_____

_____

_____

_____

_____

_____

_____

_____

_____

_____

_____

_____

_____

_____

_____

_____

_____

_____

_____

_____

WITH ALL THEIR

 HEART

 SOUL

 STRENGTH

A

Provoke
discovery

→

SO THEY WILL . . .
OWN THEIR OWN FAITH
& VALUE A FAITH COMMUNITY

 **IDENTITY**
(Coming of age)

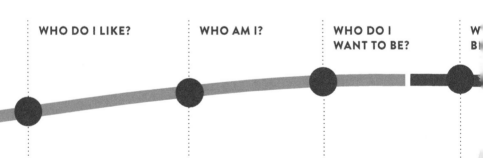

WHO DO I LIKE?	WHO AM I?	WHO DO I WANT TO BE?	W B
SIXTH	SEVENTH	EIGHTH	NI

AFFIRM their personal journey

ND trust Jesus → TO HAVE A BETTER FUTURE

Fuel

passion

→

SO THEY WILL . . .
KEEP PURSUING AUTHENTIC FAITH
& DISCOVER A PERSONAL MISSION

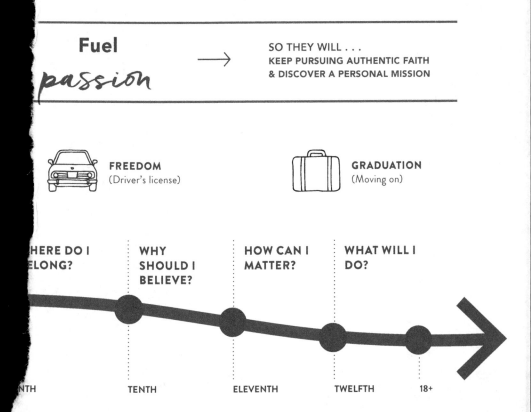

FREEDOM
(Driver's license)

GRADUATION
(Moving on)

HERE DO I
ELONG?

WHY
SHOULD I
BELIEVE?

HOW CAN I
MATTER?

WHAT WILL I
DO?

NTH

TENTH

ELEVENTH

TWELFTH

18+

MOBILIZE their potential

IT'S JUST
A PHASE
SO DON'T
MISS IT.

ABOUT THE AUTHORS

KRISTEN IVY @kristen_ivy

Kristen Ivy is executive director of the Phase Project. She and her husband, Matt, are in the preschool and elementary phases with three kids: Sawyer, Hensley, and Raleigh.

Kristen earned her Bachelors of Education from Baylor University in 2004 and received a Master of Divinity from Mercer University in 2009. She worked in the public school system as a high school biology and English teacher, where she learned firsthand the importance of influencing the next generation.

Kristen is also the executive director of messaging at Orange and has played an integral role in the development of the elementary, middle school, and high school curriculum and has shared her experiences at speaking events across the country. She is the co-author of *Playing for Keeps*, *Creating a Lead Small Culture*, *It's Just a Phase*, and *Don't Miss It*.

REGGIE JOINER @reggiejoiner

Reggie Joiner is founder and CEO of the reThink Group and co-founder of the Phase Project. He and his wife, Debbie, have reared four kids into adulthood. They now also have two grandchildren.

The reThink Group (also known as Orange) is a non-profit organization whose purpose is to influence those who influence the next generation. Orange provides resources and training for churches and organizations that create environments for parents, kids, and teenagers.

Before starting the reThink Group in 2006, Reggie was one of the founders of North Point Community Church. During his 11 years with Andy Stanley, Reggie was the executive director of family ministry, where he developed a new concept for relevant ministry to children, teenagers, and married adults. Reggie has authored and co-authored more than 10 books including: *Think Orange, Seven Practices of Effective Ministry, Parenting Beyond Your Capacity, Playing for Keeps, Lead Small, Creating a Lead Small Culture,* and his latest, *A New Kind of Leader* and *Don't Miss It.*

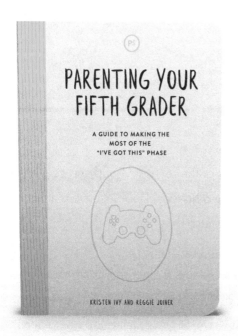

MAKE THE MOST OF EVERY PHASE IN YOUR CHILD'S LIFE

The guide in your hand is one of an eighteen-part series.

So, unless you've figured out a way to freeze time and keep your fourth grader from turning into a fifth grader, you might want to check out the next guide in this set.

Designed in partnership with Parent Cue, each guide will help you rediscover . . .

what's changing about your kid,
the 6 things your kid needs most,
and 4 conversations to have each year.

WANT TO GIFT A FRIEND WITH ALL 18 GUIDES
OR HAVE ALL THE GUIDES ON HAND FOR YOURSELF?

ORDER THE ENTIRE SERIES
OF PHASE GUIDES TODAY.